My America

A Poetry Atlas of the United States

SELECTED BY
Lee Bennett Hopkins

ILLUSTRATED BY
Stephen Alcorn

My America

A Poetry Atlas of the United States

SCHOLASTIC INC.

New York Toronto London Auckland Sydney
Mexico City New Delhi Hong Kong Buenos Aires

I wish to thank Heather Wood, art director, for inviting me to "surprise her"—an artist's dream come true if ever there was one; I also thank her for imbuing today's computer-graphics technology with a personal warmth, elegance, and intelligence that befits the poems celebrated herein. I am deeply indebted to editor Rebecca Davis, not only for her sound judgment and reassuring presence of mind, but for granting me the complete freedom to generate personal, interpretive images rather than literal transcriptions of each poem. Lastly, I take this opportunity to express my profound gratitude toward Lee Bennett Hopkins, the anthologist of this book, and Lucille Chomowicz, former art director at Simon & Schuster, for first suggesting that I should be the one to illustrate this book. —S. A.

Artist's Note

The images were painted in casein on paper, using a great variety of brushes (including an old discarded toothbrush). I worked directly on the paper, without preliminary pencil sketches. This improvisational approach enabled me to surrender to the magic of each poem. In an effort to arrive at the heart of the poems, I reworked the paintings over time, all the while building up the delicately textured surfaces you see reproduced.

To Nancy and Reath Edwards—
with a kiss-toast
from coast to coast

−L. B. H.

For Sabina, Lucrezia, and Ludovica,
aka *le tre grazie* . . .

−S. A.

CONTENTS

1 | *Introduction*

The Northeast States

2 | **Map**

3 | **Facts**

5 | **Watercolor Maine** *C. Drew Lamm*

6 | **Islands in Boston Harbor** *David McCord*

8 | **New England Lighthouse** *Rebecca Kai Dotlich*

9 | **Gulls and Buoys** *Anne LeMieux*

10 | **City Blockades** *Lee Bennett Hopkins*

11 | **Frost's Farm Road** *James Hayford*

12 | **Vermont Conversation** *Patricia Hubbell*

The Capital

14 | **Map**

15 | **Facts**

17 | **Washington, D.C.** *Rebecca Kai Dotlich*

The Southeast States

18 | **Map**

19 | **Facts**

21 | **Kentucky** *Lee Bennett Hopkins*

23 | **Knoxville, Tennessee** *Nikki Giovanni*

24 | **Bourbon and Canal** *Brod Bagert and Charles Smith*

25 | **The Mississippi** *Tom Robert Shields*

26 | **Alabama Earth**
(At Booker Washington's Grave) *Langston Hughes*

27 | **Some Rivers** *Frank Asch*

The Great Lakes States

28 | **Map**

29 | **Facts**

30 | from **Crossing Ohio When Poppies Bloom in Ashtabula** *Carl Sandburg*

31 | **This Is Indiana** *Rebecca Kai Dotlich*

32 | **Tonight in Chicago** *Anonymous*

33 | **Dear Cousin** *Kathryn Allen Ilitch*

34 | **Wisconsin in Feb-b-rr-uary** *Lee Bennett Hopkins*

35 | **Front Porch** *Leslie Nelson Jennings*

36 | **Farmer** *Prince Redcloud*

37 | **Pine Tree Tops** *Gary Snyder*

The Plains States

38 | **Map**

39 | **Facts**

40 | **Midwest Town** *Ruth De Long Peterson*

41 | **Kansas Boy** *Ruth Lechlitner*

43 | **Laughing Corn** *Carl Sandburg*

44 | **Nebraska** *Jon Swan*

45 | **Grandpa's Trees** *Barbara M. Hales*

46 | **Sioux Lullaby** *Prince Redcloud*

47 | **Winter Dark** *Lilian Moore*

The Mountain States

48 | **Map**

49 | **Facts**

50 | **"For Purple Mountains' Majesty"** *Myra Cohn Livingston*

51 | **Boulder, Colorado** *X. J. Kennedy*

52 | **Driving Montana** *Kris Aro McLeod*

53 | **Idaho** *Kaye Starbird*

54 | **Snow Country** *Dave Etter*

55 | **Skier** *Robert Francis*

56 | **Zion National Park—Utah** *Fran Haraway*

57 | **Until We Built a Cabin** *Aileen Fisher*

The Southwest States

58 | **Map**

59 | **Facts**

60 | **Lifeline** *Shonto Begay*

61 | **Cactus** *April Halprin Wayland*

63 | **Desert** *Lillian M. Fisher*

64 | **The Hawk** *Douglas Florian*

65 | **Santa Fe, New Mexico** *April Halprin Wayland*

66 | **March in New Mexico** *Elizabeth Coatsworth*

69 | **Grand Canyon Colors** *Tom Robert Shields*

The Pacific Coast States

70 | **Map**

71 | **Facts**

72 | **California Missions** *Ann Whitford Paul*

73 | **California Ghost Town** *Fran Haraway*

74 | **Behind the Redwood Curtain** *Natasha Wing*

76 | **Seattle Morning** *Lee Bennett Hopkins*

78 | **Alaska** *Joaquin Miller*

79 | **Mauna Loa** *Tom Robert Shields*

80 | *Acknowledgments*

81 | *Index of Authors*

82 | *Index of Titles*

83 | *Index of First Lines*

INTRODUCTION

Poets don't just think about America. They harbor dreams, preserve the past, reflect tomorrows by seeing, feeling, tasting, smelling, hearing—wrapping their arms around the country—with their words.

I travel extensively throughout the United States, talking with teachers, librarians, professors, parents, and children to read poetry. Whether we meet midst a bustling city, on a rich, sowed farmland, or in the smallest of villages close to somewhere yet far from anywhere, we are all Americans and we all share a love of poetry that makes our hearts beat— that joins us together—as one.

My America depicts our always forever-changing land. Through poets' voices our senses are stirred, shaken, awakened to witness the various regions that make up our great United States.

Our nation is so exciting, so multifaceted, as are poets who hail from every walk of life—who sing of cities where we "sprawl-in, sit-tall-in," areas where "wheat whirls with joyful wind," where a "mail boat chugs to the Cranberry Islands" of Maine.

Poets reveal the diversity of our nation's people, too—a Kansas boy who never saw the sea, a Native American child singing a lullaby to his little brother, a farmer and his wife talking things over together.

Poets praise our country's natural wonders—the Grand Canyon, the Everglades, the mighty Mississippi River—as well as tucked away, remote places like a California ghost town, "a village / where lighted streets were few," an ice mountain "hurled / Down this unfinished world." Poets also voice the ordinary—a pebble pocketed from a farm, ripening wheat, lazy ants.

My America, divided into eight sections, one for each unique region, captures the breadth, depth, and character of the United States. Prefacing each section are fascinating facts about each state and the Capital.

Twenty new commissioned works appear along with a host of beloved poets—including Langston Hughes, X. J. Kennedy, David McCord, and Carl Sandburg—to bring the United States into a distinctive focus.

Stephen Alcorn's powerful paintings add further dimension, interpreting the works with brilliant design, color, and composition.

My America pays a fitting tribute to our nation. Journey through our incredible country—from the coast of Maine to the Hawaiian Islands. It's a trip you'll want to take over and over again.

— Lee Bennett Hopkins
SCARBOROUGH, NEW YORK

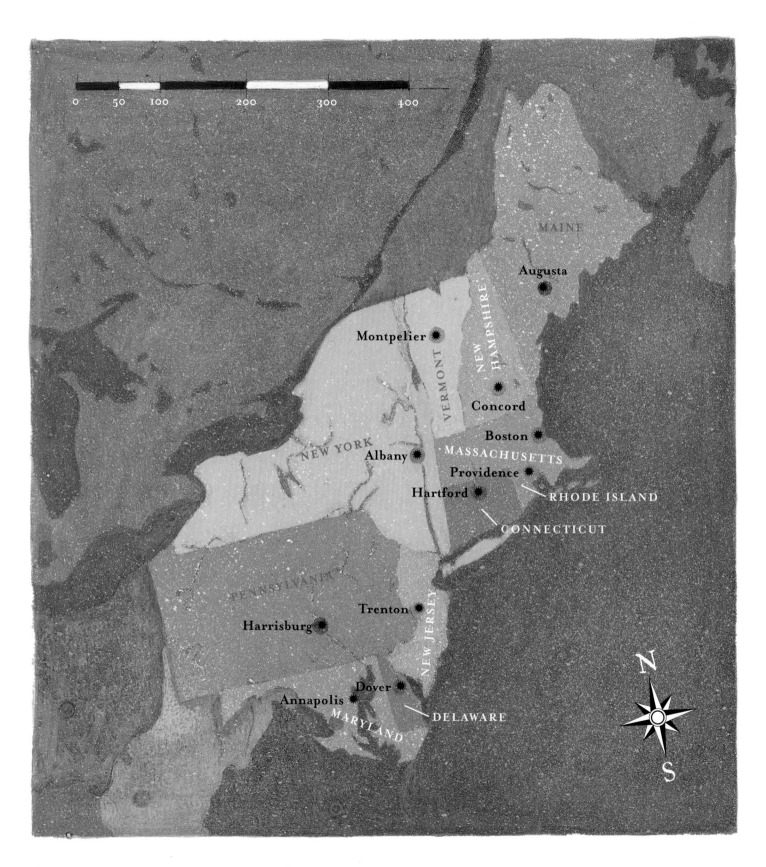

THE NORTHEAST STATES

CONNECTICUT
CT

On January 9, 1788, Connecticut became the fifth state to ratify the Constitution.

Capital: Hartford
Nickname: Constitution State/Nutmeg State
Motto: *Qui Transtulit Sustinet*
He Who Transplanted Still Sustains
Bird: American Robin
Flower: Mountain Laurel
Tree: White Oak
Area: 5,544 square miles; rank 48

Great Fact:
Founded in 1764, the *Hartford Courant* is the oldest continuously published newspaper in the United States.

DELAWARE
DE

On December 7, 1787, Delaware became the first state to ratify the Constitution.

Capital: Dover
Nickname: First State/Diamond State
Motto: *Liberty and Independence*
Bird: Blue Hen Chicken
Flower: Peach Blossom
Tree: American Holly
Area: 2,397 square miles; rank 49

Great Fact:
Log cabins were first introduced to North America in the early 1600s in Delaware. They were constructed by Swedes and Finns who settled near the mouth of the Delaware River.

MAINE
ME

On March 15, 1820, Maine became the twenty-third state.

Capital: Augusta
Nickname: Pine Tree State
Motto: *Dirigo*
I Direct or I Guide
Bird: Black-Capped Chickadee
Flower: White Pine Cone and Tassel
Tree: Eastern White Pine
Area: 33,741 square miles; rank 39

Great Fact:
More wooden toothpicks are produced in Maine than in any other state. The wood for the toothpicks comes from white birch.

MARYLAND
MD

On April 28, 1788, Maryland became the seventh state to ratify the Constitution.

Capital: Annapolis
Nickname: Old Line State/Free State
Motto: *Fatti Maschii, Parole Femine*
Manly Deeds, Womanly Words
Bird: Baltimore Oriole
Flower: Black-Eyed Susan
Tree: White Oak
Area: 12,297 square miles; rank 42

Great Fact:
The largest white oak tree in the United States is the Wye Oak in Wye Mills. This 107-foot-tall tree has a circumference of 34 1/2 feet at the trunk's base, and is more than 450 years old.

MASSACHUSETTS
MA

On February 6, 1788, Massachusetts became the sixth state to ratify the Constitution.

Capital: Boston
Nickname: Bay State/Old Colony State
Motto: *Ense Petit Placidam Sub Libertate Quietem*
By the Sword We Seek Peace, but Peace Only Under Liberty
Bird: Black-Capped Chickadee
Flower: Mayflower/Trailing Arbutus
Tree: American Elm
Area: 9,241 square miles; rank 45

Great Fact:
The first baseball World Series games were played between the National League and American League champions from October 1 to October 13, 1903, in Boston. The Boston Pilgrims defeated the Pittsburgh Pirates.

NEW HAMPSHIRE
NH

On June 21, 1788, New Hampshire became the ninth state to ratify the Constitution.

Capital: Concord
Nickname: Granite State
Motto: *Live Free or Die*
Bird: Purple Finch
Flower: Purple Lilac
Tree: White Birch
Area: 9,283 square miles; rank 44

Great Fact:
In 1961, Alan B. Shepard, Jr., born in East Derry, became the first American to travel into space in a capsule named *Freedom 7*.

NEW JERSEY
NJ

On December 18, 1787, New Jersey became the third state to ratify the Constitution.

Capital: Trenton
Nickname: Garden State
Motto: *Liberty and Prosperity*
Bird: Eastern Goldfinch
Flower: Purple Violet
Tree: Red Oak
Area: 8,215 square miles; rank 46

Great Fact:
In the early 1900s, at the time Thomas Alva Edison was pioneering the development of motion picture equipment in his laboratory in Menlo Park, the film capital of the world was Fort Lee. With his invention of the kinetoscope in 1888, Edison had launched a new era of entertainment throughout the entire world.

NEW YORK
NY

On July 26, 1788, New York became the eleventh state to ratify the Constitution.

Capital: Albany
Nickname: Empire State
Motto: *Excelsior*
Ever Upward
Bird: Bluebird
Flower: Rose
Tree: Sugar Maple
Area: 53,989 square miles; rank 27

Great Fact:
Radio City Music Hall in New York City is the world's largest indoor theater. It has a seating capacity of 5,900.

PENNSYLVANIA
PA

On December 12, 1787, Pennsylvania became the second state to ratify the Constitution.

Capital: Harrisburg
Nickname: Keystone State
Motto: *Virtue, Liberty, and Independence*
Bird: Ruffed Grouse
Flower: Mountain Laurel
Tree: Hemlock
Area: 45,759 square miles; rank 33

Great Fact:
The world's largest chocolate factory, the Hershey Plant in Hershey, was established in 1903.

RHODE ISLAND
RI

On May 29, 1790, Rhode Island became the thirteenth state to ratify the Constitution.

Capital: Providence
Nickname: Little Rhody/Ocean State
Motto: *Hope*
Bird: Rhode Island Red
Flower: Purple Violet
Tree: Red Maple
Area: 1,231 square miles; rank 50

Great Fact:
The chicken called the Rhode Island Red made poultry-raising a major industry in the United States. Developed in 1854, the breed, raised on a farm in Little Compton, became famous for its delicious meat as well as its quality and quantity of eggs.

VERMONT
VT

On March 4, 1791, Vermont became the fourteenth state to ratify the Constitution.

Capital: Montpelier
Nickname: Green Mountain State
Motto: *Freedom and Unity*
Bird: Hermit Thrush
Flower: Red Clover
Tree: Sugar Maple
Area: 9,615 square miles; rank 43

Great Fact:
Vermont is the largest producer of maple sugar and syrup in the United States.

Watercolor Maine   *C. Drew Lamm*

The buoy bell sings Bar Harbor
sings the coast of Maine
to the fog.

Lobsters clap in traps.
The great quartz rocks
twist waves into fireworks.

Red lobster boats bob above barnacled anchors.
Blueberries sprinkle the shore.
Mail boat chugs to the Cranberry Islands,
Captain's black coffee rocks on the floor.

Morning light wakens the edges of bells
whets the rock and
sea.

Just another Monday Maine day waking.
The painter lifts her brush and starts her painting.

Islands in Boston Harbor   *David McCord*

How many islands in the bay?
About a hundred, so they say.
I hope they'll all be there today!

Few people know them. Few can boast
They've been on one and seen the ghost
Of Captain Kidd perhaps—almost.

Down on the map they look so queer:
Unvisited, remote and drear,
They might be miles away from here.

Down on the map you can't see where
The pirates hid, when they were there.
One island looks just like a pair

Of spectacles; one's like a whale,
And one's a fish without a tail,
And one's a ship without a sail.

Still others seem what they are not:
Napoleon's boot, the moon and what
Might be a fat smoked ham. A lot

Is in one island's point of view:
The boat I'm on will pass a few.
You look at them. They look at you.

The best have beaches, trees, and rocks,
And cormorants, and gulls in flocks;
But some are faced with granite blocks

Where ancient forts for guns and stuff
Were used by us when times were tough.
Of islands, who can have enough?

Some day a boat will land me right
Upon the shore of one—it might.
And would *I* be a welcome sight!

Just all that island: none but me,
Exploring everything—free, free!
And everywhere—the sea, the sea!

New England Lighthouse

Rebecca Kai Dotlich

It's a tower
of stone,
a refuge of white
with a code
all its own,
flashing constant
and bright.
It's a house
made of iron,
a home of
concrete;
a vigilant
beacon
for sailors
at sea.
It's a turret
of lanterns;
a castle of lights—
a compass for ships
as they pass
through the night.

Gulls and Buoys   *Anne LeMieux*

Gulls swoop, gulls soar,
Flocking, flying, gulls galore.
Gulls wheel, gulls wing,
Clamorous chorus, gulls sing.
Gulls squawk, gulls screech
By the buoys, on the beach.
Gulls gather, gulls together,
Raucous caucus, birds of a feather.

City Blockades   *Lee Bennett Hopkins*

I feel so small
standing beneath the tall
buildings that wall
me and the pigeons in
from the light of the
sky.

Frost's Farm Road
James Hayford

I pocketed a pebble
From Frost's farm road at Ripton,
Not because it differed much
In looks from my home pebbles,
But because maybe his shoe
Might have stepped on or near it,
Or his eye noticed it,
Or cars from Washington,
New York, Hanover, Cambridge
Passed over or beside it,
In that high circle of his
In or just under the Great World.

Vermont Conversation

Patricia Hubbell

"Good weather for hay."
  "Yes, 'tis."
"Mighty bright day."
  "That's true."
"Crops comin' on?"
  "Yep. You?"
"Tol'rable; beans got the blight."
  "Way o' the Lord."
"That's right."

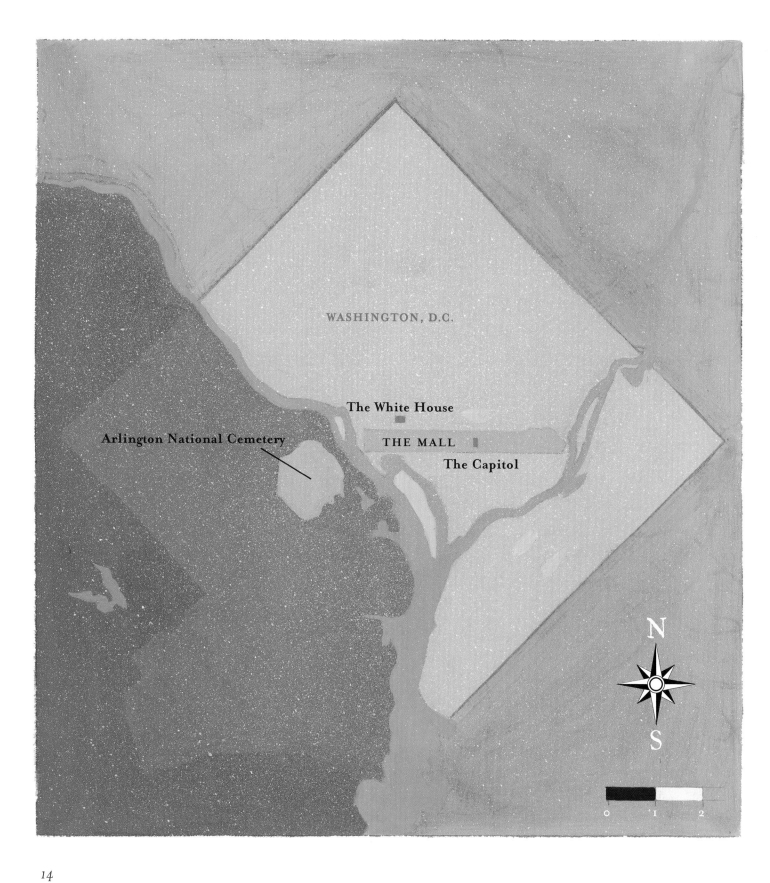

WASHINGTON, D.C.

The White House

THE MALL

The Capitol

Arlington National Cemetery

N

S

0   1   2

THE CAPITAL

WASHINGTON, D.C.

The District of Columbia is not a state; it is the seat of the United States Federal Government. The United States Constitution provided that an area of land be set aside for the nation's capital. Authorized by Congress in 1790, George Washington named the choice of this location in 1791, appointing Pierre Charles L'Enfant, a French architect, to plan the capital on an area not more than 10 miles square. In 1800 the Federal Government moved the capital from Philadelphia, Pennsylvania. The City of Washington was incorporated in 1802. The District of Columbia was originally made up of portions of land from Maryland and Virginia; the Virginia land portion was returned to the state in 1846. Today, Washington, D.C., is among the most important centers of government in the world.

Motto:	*Justitia Omnibus*
	Justice to All
Bird:	Wood Thrush
Flower:	American Beauty Rose
Tree:	Scarlet Oak
Area:	68 square miles; rank 51

Great Fact:
The Vietnam Veterans Memorial was built in 1982 by Maya Lin, an American sculptor and architect. The wall is inscribed with names of more than 58,000 Americans killed or missing during the Vietnam War (1954–1975).

Washington, D.C. *Rebecca Kai Dotlich*

On the east bank of the Potomac,
lies Washington, D.C.
the capital of our Nation
which stands for liberty.

It's here our U.S. Presidents
are sworn into command;
where the courtly U.S. Capitol
and the stately White House stand.

Sweet cherry blossoms spice the air
of city blocks in patterned squares,
and grassy knolls and splendid parks
claim rare museums and grand landmarks.

Where patriotic monuments
stand haunting in the night;
where King proclaimed, *I have a dream,*
and Kennedy's flame burns bright.

It's here, in a place called Arlington,
where stars and stripes do fly;
where silent snow-white tombstones march
in rows where heroes lie.

The Tomb of the Unknown Soldier;
the changing of the guard.
The gardens and the galleries,
the tree-lined boulevards.

From around the world they come to touch
with tears and hushed acclaim
the sleek and sacred granite Wall
engraved with soldiers' names.

On the east bank of the Potomac,
lies Washington, D.C.
the capital of our Nation
which stands for liberty.

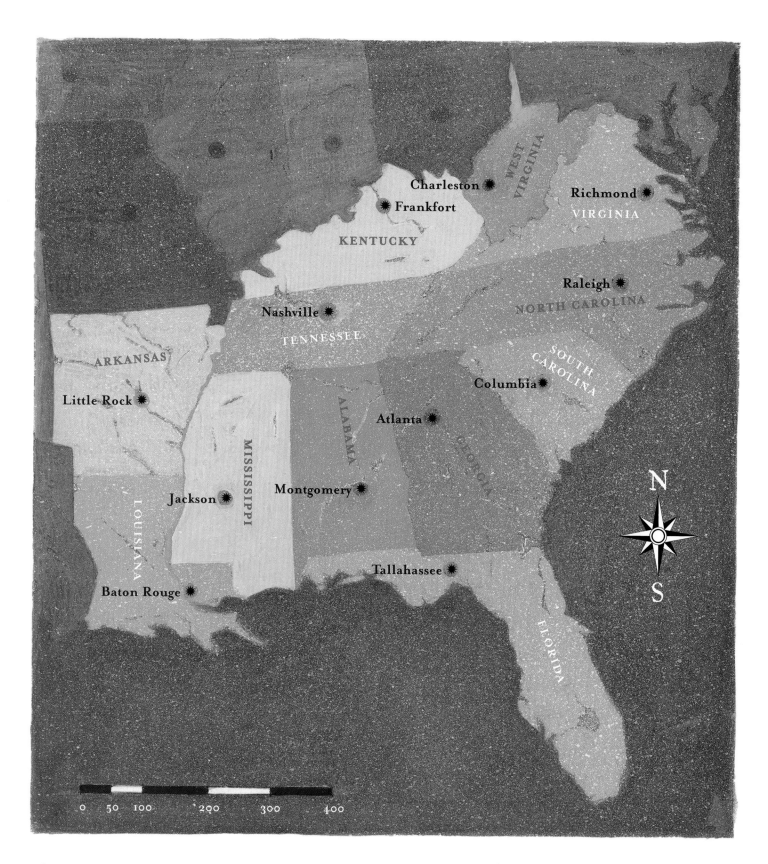

Charleston

Frankfort

WEST VIRGINIA

Richmond

VIRGINIA

KENTUCKY

Raleigh

NORTH CAROLINA

Nashville

TENNESSEE

ARKANSAS

SOUTH CAROLINA

Columbia

Little Rock

Atlanta

ALABAMA

MISSISSIPPI

GEORGIA

Jackson

Montgomery

LOUISIANA

Tallahassee

N

S

Baton Rouge

FLORIDA

0   50   100   200   300   400

THE SOUTHEAST STATES

ALABAMA

On December 14, 1819, Alabama became the twenty-second state.

Capital:	Montgomery
Nickname:	Cotton State/Heart of Dixie
Motto:	*We Dare Defend Our Rights*
Bird:	Yellowhammer
Flower:	Camellia
Tree:	Southern Pine
Area:	52,237 square miles; rank 30

Great Fact:

Tuskegee University in Tuskegee, one of the nation's oldest seats of learning for African Americans, was founded on July 4, 1881, by Booker Taliaferro Washington.

ARKANSAS

On June 15, 1836, Arkansas became the twenty-fifth state.

Capital:	Little Rock
Nickname:	Land of Opportunity
Motto:	*Regnat Populus*
	The People Rule
Bird:	Mockingbird
Flower:	Apple Blossom
Tree:	Ponderosa Pine
Area:	53,182 square miles; rank 28

Great Fact:

America's largest federal trout hatchery is the Norfolk National Fish Hatchery in Mountain Home. More than 2 million trout are raised here each year until they are about 9 inches long. The fish are then placed in streams in Arkansas, Missouri, and Oklahoma.

FLORIDA

On March 3, 1845, Florida became the twenty-seventh state.

Capital:	Tallahassee
Nickname:	Sunshine State
Motto:	*In God We Trust*
Bird:	Mockingbird
Flower:	Orange Blossom
Tree:	Sabal Palmetto Palm
Area:	59,988 square miles; rank 24

Great Fact:

On July 16, 1969, at 9:32 A.M., *Apollo 11*, the first spacecraft to land astronauts on the moon, was launched from Cape Canaveral, then called Cape Kennedy.

GEORGIA

On January 2, 1788, Georgia became the fourth state to ratify the Constitution.

Capital:	Atlanta
Nickname:	Empire State of the
	South/Peach State
Motto:	*Wisdom, Justice,*
	Moderation
Bird:	Brown Thrasher
Flower:	Cherokee Rose
Tree:	Live Oak
Area:	58,977 square miles; rank 24

Great Fact:

The Girl Scouts of the U.S.A. was founded by Juliette Gordon Low of Savannah on March 12, 1912. Low's childhood home is now the Girl Scout National Center, one of Savannah's National Historic Landmarks.

KENTUCKY

On June 1, 1792, Kentucky became the fifteenth state.

Capital:	Frankfort
Nickname:	Bluegrass State
Motto:	*United We Stand, Divided*
	We Fall
Bird:	Cardinal
Flower:	Goldenrod
Tree:	Kentucky Coffeetree
Area:	40,411 square miles; rank 37

Great Fact:

Part of the Mammoth Cave National Park, the Mammoth-Flint Ridge cave system is the largest known in the world. The system is more than 300 miles long.

LOUISIANA

On April 30, 1812, Louisiana became the eighteenth state.

Capital:	Baton Rouge
Nickname:	Pelican State
Motto:	*Union, Justice, Confidence*
Bird:	Brown Pelican
Flower:	Magnolia
Tree:	Bald Cypress
Area:	49,650 square miles; rank 31

Great Fact:

A total of 87 percent of all crayfish produced in the United States comes from Louisiana—more than any other place in the world. Nearly 125,000 acres are devoted to raising crayfish as a seafood delicacy.

MISSISSIPPI

MS

On December 10, 1817, Mississippi became the twentieth state.

Capital:	Jackson
Nickname:	Magnolia State
Motto:	*Virtute et Armis*
	By Valor and Arms
Bird:	Mockingbird
Flower:	Magnolia
Tree:	Magnolia
Area:	48,236 square miles; rank 32

Great Fact:

Hiram R. Revels became the first African American to be elected to the United States Senate on February 25, 1870.

NORTH CAROLINA

NC

On November 21, 1789, North Carolina became the twelfth state to ratify the Constitution.

Capital:	Raleigh
Nickname:	Tar Heel State/Old North State
Motto:	*Esse Quam Videri*
	To Be Rather Than to Seem
Bird:	Cardinal
Flower:	Flowering Dogwood
Tree:	Ponderosa Pine
Area:	52,672 square miles; rank 29

Great Fact:

Virginia Dare was the first English child to be born in America on Roanoke Island on August 18, 1587. Her parents were Ananias Dare and Ellinor White, two members of a band of 117 colonists who settled on Roanoke Island. Little else is known about Virginia Dare, since the colony into which she was born mysteriously disappeared.

SOUTH CAROLINA

SC

On May 23, 1788, South Carolina became the eighth state to ratify the Constitution.

Capital:	Columbia
Nickname:	Palmetto State
Motto:	*Dum Spiro, Spero/*
	Animis Opibusque Parati
	While I Breathe, I Hope/
	Prepared in Mind and Resources
Bird:	Carolina Wren
Flower:	Yellow Jessamine
Tree:	Palmetto
Area:	31,189 square miles; rank 40

Great Fact:

Houses called "hearts of pine" built during colonial times still stand today. During the state's early days timber was so plentiful that "sapwood" was discarded and only the hearts of pine trees were used. The wood is said to last indefinitely.

TENNESSEE

TN

On June 1, 1796, Tennessee became the sixteenth state.

Capital:	Nashville
Nickname:	Volunteer State
Motto:	*Agriculture and Commerce*
Bird:	Mockingbird
Flower:	Iris
Tree:	Tulip Poplar
Area:	42,145 square miles; rank 36

Great Fact:

Tennessee's largest lake, Reelfoot, near Tiptonville, was formed by an earthquake in 1811.

VIRGINIA

VA

On June 25, 1788, Virginia became the tenth state to ratify the Constitution.

Capital:	Richmond
Nickname:	Old Dominion/Mother of Presidents
Motto:	*Sic Semper Tyrannis*
	Thus Always to Tyrants
Bird:	Cardinal
Flower:	Flowering Dogwood
Tree:	Dogwood
Area:	42,326 square miles; rank 35

Great Fact:

The only life-size statue of George Washington, the nation's first president, was created in marble by Jean-Antoine Houdon, a French sculptor. The statue was placed in the rotunda of the Virginia State Capitol in Richmond in 1796.

WEST VIRGINIA

WV

On June 20, 1863, West Virginia became the thirty-fifth state.

Capital:	Charleston
Nickname:	Mountain State
Motto:	*Montani Semper Liberi*
	Mountaineers Are Always Free
Bird:	Cardinal
Flower:	Big Rhododendron
Tree:	Sugar Maple
Area:	24,232 square miles; rank 41

Great Fact:

Several factories in the Parkersburg area of West Virginia produce most of the nation's glass marbles.

Kentucky

Lee Bennett Hopkins

Come on along—
Be happy-go-lucky.
Come on along—
To old Kentucky

Where you can rap
'Bout Cumberland Gap—
And watch the bluegrass flow—
And think of Boone
And the trails he'd blaze—
And behold prized Thoroughbreds
As they pasture-graze.

Come on along—
Be happy-go-lucky.
Come on along—
To old Kentucky.

Knoxville, Tennessee

Nikki Giovanni

i always like summer
best
you can eat fresh corn
from daddy's garden
and okra
and greens
and cabbage
and lots of
barbecue
and buttermilk
and homemade ice-cream
at the church picnic
and listen to
gospel music
outside
at the church
homecoming
and go to the mountains with
your grandmother
and go barefooted
and be warm
all the time
not only when you go to bed
and sleep

Bourbon and Canal   *Brod Bagert and Charles Smith*

Corner of Bourbon and Canal,
That's where she said we'd meet.
So just which ten of these 50,000 toes
Belongs to her two feet?

The Mississippi   *Tom Robert Shields*

Two thousand
Three hundred
Forty miles
Of an old flowing show.

Steamboats still steam.
Showboats glow.

And—

On a raft forever—ever—
Huckleberry Finn—
mysterious—

Somewhere—
Somewhere—
Deep, deep within.

Alabama Earth
(At Booker Washington's Grave)

Langston Hughes

Deep in Alabama earth
His buried body lies—
But higher than the singing pines
And taller than the skies
And out of Alabama earth
To all the world there goes
The truth a simple heart has held
And the strength a strong hand knows,
While over Alabama earth
These words are gently spoken:
Serve—and hate will die unborn.
Love—and chains are broken.

Some Rivers

Frank Asch

Some rivers rush to the sea.
They push and tumble and fall.
But the Everglades is a river
with no hurry in her at all.
Soaking the cypress
that grows so tall;
nursing a frog,
so quiet and small;
she flows but a mile
in the course of a day,
with plenty of time
to think on the way.

But how can she cope
with the acres of corn
and sorrowful cities that drain her?
With hunters and tourists and levees
that chain and stain and pain her?
Does the half of her that's left
think only of the past?
Or does she think of her future
and how long it will last?
Some rivers rush to the sea.
They push and tumble and fall.
But the Everglades is a river
with no hurry in her at all.

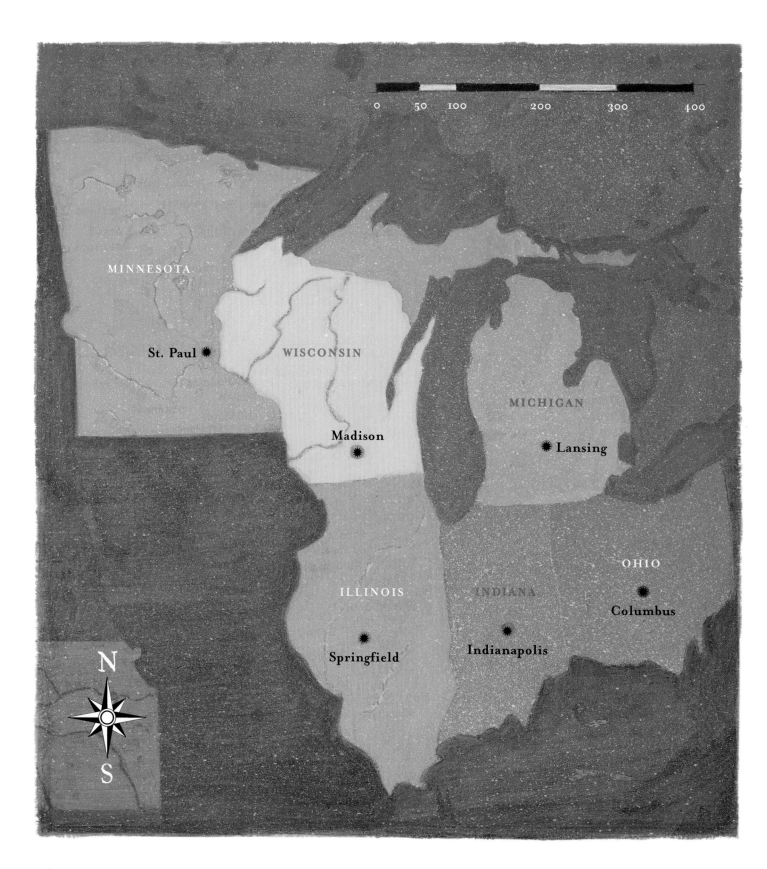

0 50 100 200 300 400

MINNESOTA

St. Paul ✳

WISCONSIN

Madison ✳

MICHIGAN

✳ Lansing

ILLINOIS

INDIANA

OHIO

Columbus ✳

Springfield ✳

Indianapolis ✳

N
S

28

THE GREAT LAKES STATES

ILLINOIS

On December 3, 1818, Illinois became the twenty-first state.

Capital: Springfield
Nickname: Prairie State
Motto: *State Sovereignty—National Union*
Bird: Cardinal
Flower: Native Violet
Tree: White Oak
Area: 57,918 square miles; rank 25

Great Fact:
On May 3, 1973, the Sears Tower in Chicago became the world's tallest building. It rises 110 stories to a height of 1,454 feet.

INDIANA

On December 11, 1816, Indiana became the nineteenth state.

Capital: Indianapolis
Nickname: Hoosier State
Motto: *The Crossroads of America*
Bird: Cardinal
Flower: Peony
Tree: Tulip Poplar
Area: 36,420 square miles; rank 38

Great Fact:
Santa Claus, a village in Indiana, receives more than 1/2 million packages, letters, and cards for remailing during each Christmas season. Named in 1852, the village has the only United States post office with the name Santa Claus.

MICHIGAN

On January 26, 1837, Michigan became the twenty-sixth state.

Capital: Lansing
Nickname: Wolverine State/Lake State
Motto: *Si Quaeris Peninsulam Amoenam, Circumspice If You Seek a Pleasant Peninsula, Look About You*
Bird: Robin
Flower: Apple Blossom
Tree: White Pine
Area: 96,705 square miles; rank 11

Great Fact:
Battle Creek, nicknamed "The Cereal Bowl of America," produces more breakfast cereal than any other city in the world.

MINNESOTA

On May 11, 1858, Minnesota became the thirty-second state.

Capital: St. Paul
Nickname: North Star State/Gopher State/Land of 10,000 Lakes
Motto: *L'étoile du Nord Star of the North*
Bird: Common Loon
Flower: Pink and White Lady's Slipper
Tree: Red Pine
Area: 86,942 square miles; rank 12

Great Fact:
Cellophane transparent tape was invented and patented by Richard Gurley Drew of St. Paul. The Minnesota Manufacturing Company began producing the tape in 1930.

OHIO

On March 1, 1803, Ohio became the seventeenth state.

Capital: Columbus
Nickname: Buckeye State
Motto: *With God, All Things Are Possible*
Bird: Cardinal
Flower: Scarlet Carnation
Tree: Buckeye
Area: 44,828 square miles; rank 34

Great Fact:
The first electric traffic signal lights on record in the United States were placed on Euclid Avenue and E. 105th Street in Cleveland on August 5, 1914. Invented by James Hoge of Cleveland, the original traffic signals had bells that rang to warn motorists when the lights were about to change.

WISCONSIN

On May 29, 1848, Wisconsin became the thirtieth state.

Capital: Madison
Nickname: Badger State
Motto: *Forward*
Bird: Robin
Flower: Wood Violet
Tree: Sugar Maple
Area: 65,500 square miles; rank 22

Great Fact:
William Horlick invented malted milk in 1887 in Racine.

from Crossing Ohio When Poppies Bloom in Ashtabula

Carl Sandburg

Pick me poppies in Ohio,
mother.
Pick me poppies in a back yard
in Ashtabula.
May going, poppies coming, summer humming:
make it a poppy summer, mother; the leaves
sing in the silk, the leaves sing a tawny
red gold; seven sunsets saved themselves
to be here now.

Pick me poppies, mother; go, May; wash me,
summer; shoot up this back yard in Ashtabula, shoot it up, give us a daylight fireworks in Ohio, burn it up with tawny red
gold.

This Is Indiana

Rebecca Kai Dotlich

This is Indiana,
the place that I love—
with wide open spaces
and stars above.
It's a bountiful wheat,
sweet corn growing land;
home of James Whitcomb Riley
and his *Raggedy Man.*

This is Indiana,
where the Wabash flows;
where the steel mills stand,
and the tulip tree grows.
Where the limestone quarries
for buildings reside,
and the Indy 500
is known worldwide.

This is Indiana,
veined with fields and farms.
Scored with rivers and lakes,
paved with bridges and barns.
Embroidered with churches
on rich, fertile land—
in a homeland of Hoosiers,

and basketball fans!

Tonight in Chicago

Anonymous

It's a sitting-pretty, windy-city kind of a place.
It's a dine-au-château, lake-shore-below,
Kind of a place.
It's the Loop and the Mart, a great city's heart;
It's a quiet-and-gentle, elegantal, Continental
Kind of a place.
A sprawl-in, sit-tall-in kind of a place.

A quiet lair, a want-to-be-there, a welcome fa
Kind of a place.
It's a tall-one-all-tinkly, a smile-all-wrinkly,
It's a wonderful food, wonderful mood,
Kind of a place.
It's excitement and fun, adventure begun, a
Candlelight and spotlight
Kind of a place.

Dear Cousin

Kathryn Allen Ilitch

Dear Cousin:

Next time I visit Michigan I sure would like to fish again!
It doesn't matter on which lake
or stream
or pond—
make no mistake—
I love to fish!
The hooks! The bait! The nets! The fun! I just can't wait!

I promise that I will not squirm
or scream
next time I touch a worm.
I'll hold it tight. I'll even look.
I'll wrap that thing around the hook.
I promise I won't make you do it.
"Ta da!" I'll say. "There's nothing to it!"
I swear I'll be a helpful elf—
I'll watch my bobber by myself
until it bobs right out of sight
and then,
if you don't mind, I might
just ask you
one
last
little
favor
(because you are a little braver):
next time I visit Michigan, will you unhook my fish again?

Wisconsin in Feb-b-rr-uary

Lee Bennett Hopkins

B-rr, b-rr, b-rr, b-rr,
b-rr, b-rr, b-rr, b-rr,
b-rr, b-rr, b-rr, b-rr,
b-rr, b-rr, b-rr, b-rr,
b-rr, b-rr, b-rr, b-rr,
b-rr, b-rr, b-rr, b-rr,
b-rr, b-rr, b-rr, b-rr,
b-rr, b-rr, b-rr, b-rr,
b-rr, b-rr, b-rr, b-rr,
b-rr, b-rr, b-rr, b-rr:

huff
puff
rough
tough

enough
of
Feb-b-rr-uary!

34

Front Porch · *Leslie Nelson Jennings*

People who live in cities never know
  The creak of hickory rockers and the hum
Of talk about what happened years ago.
  Just sitting on the sunny side of some
Old house can bring us closer to events
  Than counting seconds, though the world says not.
If looking backward doesn't make good sense
  Tomorrow, then, may be as well forgot.

Those who planned farmsteads hereabouts took time
  Enough to square a beam and see it placed.
A man of sixty wasn't past his prime
  And nothing worth a penny went to waste.
We can remember many things with pride,
Who built front porches neighborly and wide.

Farmer *Prince Redcloud*

The farmer, worn from
long field-days, trods home to a
welcome, warm supper.

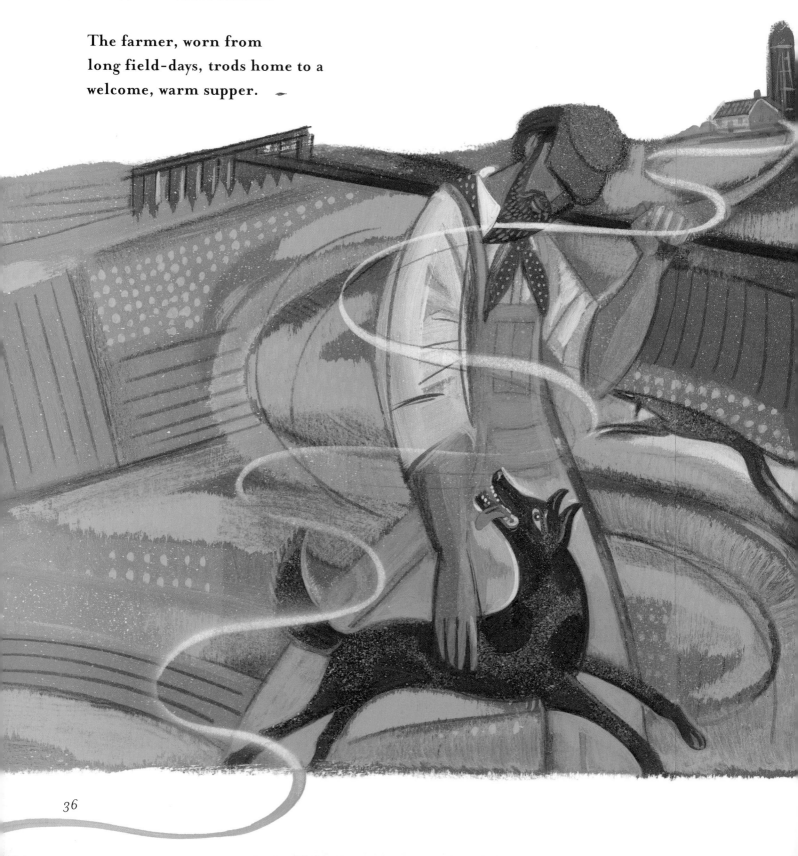

Pine Tree Tops

Gary Snyder

in the blue night
frost haze, the sky glows
with the moon
pine tree tops
bend snow-blue, fade
into sky, frost, starlight.
the creak of boots.
rabbit tracks, deer tracks,
what do we know.

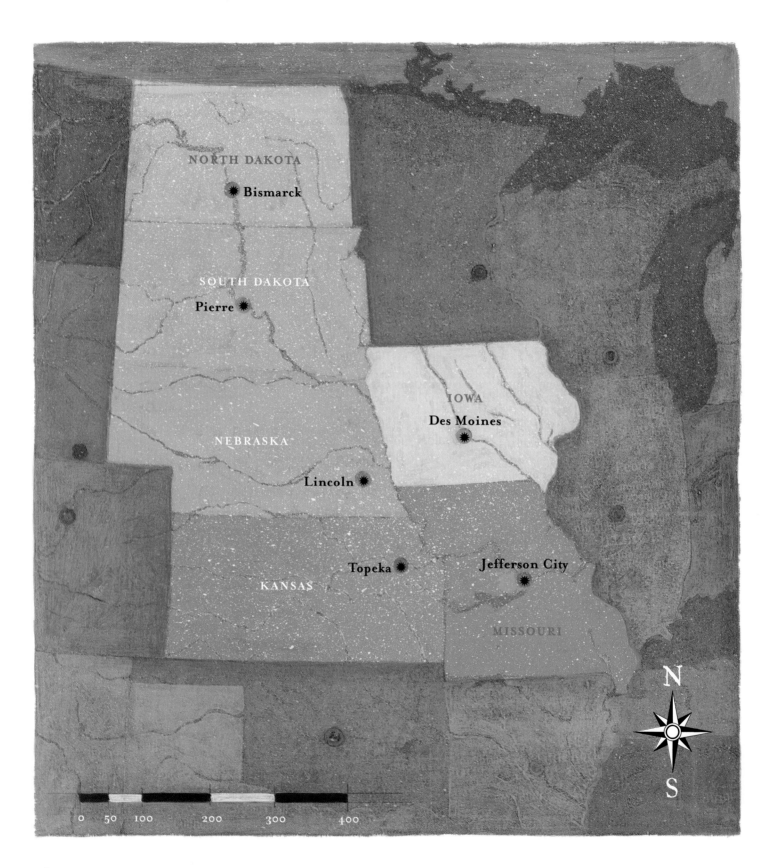

NORTH DAKOTA

Bismarck

SOUTH DAKOTA

Pierre

IOWA

Des Moines

NEBRASKA

Lincoln

Topeka

Jefferson City

KANSAS

MISSOURI

N

S

0   50   100   200   300   400

THE PLAINS STATES

IOWA

IA

On December 28, 1846, Iowa became the twenty-ninth state.

Capital: Des Moines
Nickname: Hawkeye State
Motto: *Our Liberties We Prize and Our Rights We Will Maintain*
Bird: Eastern Goldfinch
Flower: Wild Rose
Tree: Oak
Area: 56,276 square miles; rank 26

Great Fact:
One of the top-selling apples in the United States, the Red Delicious, was developed on an orchard near the town of East Peru, owned by Jesse Hiatt, in the 1880s. Hiatt called the apple "Hawkeye." In 1895, Stark Brothers Nursery purchased rights to the apple, renaming it "Delicious." Offshoots of the original tree still produce apples on the same orchard where it began.

KANSAS

KS

On January 29, 1861, Kansas became the thirty-fourth state.

Capital: Topeka
Nickname: Sunflower State
Motto: *Ad Astra per Aspera To the Stars Through Difficulties*
Bird: Western Meadowlark
Flower: Sunflower
Tree: Cottonwood
Area: 82,282 square miles; rank 15

Great Fact:
In 1886, Susanna Salter became the first woman mayor in the United States. She was elected in the town of Argonia. The election also marked the first time women in Kansas were allowed to vote in city elections.

MISSOURI

MO

On August 10, 1821, Missouri became the twenty-fourth state.

Capital: Jefferson City
Nickname: Show Me State
Motto: *Salus Populi Suprema Lex Esto The Welfare of the People Shall Be the Supreme Law*
Bird: Bluebird
Flower: Hawthorn
Tree: Dogwood
Area: 69,709 square miles; rank 21

Great Fact:
Ice-cream cones were first served in 1904 in St. Louis at the Louisiana Purchase Exposition world's fair.

NEBRASKA

NE

On March 1, 1867, Nebraska became the thirty-seventh state.

Capital: Lincoln
Nickname: Cornhusker State
Motto: *Equality Before the Law*
Bird: Western Meadowlark
Flower: Goldenrod
Tree: Cottonwood
Area: 77,359 square miles; rank 16

Great Fact:
Concerned about Nebraska's lack of tree growth, Julius Sterling Morton, a newspaper publisher, convinced the state's agricultural board to set aside a special day for tree-planting. April 10, 1872, became the first Arbor Day in the United States. It was such a success that more than a million trees were planted. Since that date, Arbor Day has become a nationwide holiday.

NORTH DAKOTA

ND

On November 2, 1889, North Dakota became the thirty-ninth state.

Capital: Bismarck
Nickname: Peach Garden State/Sioux State/Flickertail State
Motto: *Liberty and Union, Now and Forever, One and Inseparable*
Bird: Western Meadowlark
Flower: Wild Prairie Rose
Tree: American Elm
Area: 70,704 square miles; rank 18

Great Fact:
Petroleum became the state's most valuable mineral when oil was discovered near Tioga in 1951. By 1970, oil wells were operating in 14 counties in western North Dakota.

SOUTH DAKOTA
SD

On November 2, 1889, South Dakota became the fortieth state.

Capital: Pierre
Nickname: Coyote State/Mount Rushmore State
Motto: *Under God the People Rule*
Bird: Chinese Ring-Necked Pheasant
Flower: Pasqueflower
Tree: Black Hills Spruce
Area: 77,121 square miles; rank 17

Great Fact:
The Mount Rushmore National Memorial in the Black Hills is the largest sculpture in the world. It depicts the heads of four United States presidents—George Washington, Abraham Lincoln, Thomas Jefferson, and Theodore Roosevelt. Millions of tourists visit the site each year.

Midwest Town

Ruth De Long Peterson

Farther east it wouldn't be on the map—
    Too small—but here it rates a dot and a name.
In Europe it would wear a castle cap
    Or have a cathedral rising like a flame.

But here it stands where the section roadways meet.
    Its houses dignified with trees and lawn;
The stores hold *tête-à-tête* across Main Street;
    The red brick school, a church—the town is gone.

America is not all traffic lights,
    And beehive homes and shops and factories;
No, there are wide green days and starry nights,
    And a great pulse beating strong in towns like these.

Kansas Boy

Ruth Lechlitner

This Kansas boy who never saw the sea
Walks through the young corn rippling at his knee
As sailors walk; and when the grain grows higher
Watches the dark waves leap with greener fire
Than ever oceans hold. He follows ships,
Tasting the bitter spray upon his lips,
For in his blood up-stirs the salty ghost
Of one who sailed a storm-bound English coast.
Across wide fields he hears the sea winds crying,
Shouts at the crows—and dreams of white
    gulls flying.

Laughing Corn

Carl Sandburg

There was a high majestic fooling
Day before yesterday in the yellow corn.

And day after tomorrow in the yellow corn
There will be high majestic fooling.

The ears ripen in late summer
And come on with a conquering laughter,
Come on with a high and conquering laughter.

The long-tailed blackbirds are hoarse.
One of the smaller blackbirds chitters on a stalk
And a spot of red is on its shoulder
And I never heard its name in my life.

Some of the ears are bursting.
A white juice works inside.
Cornsilk creeps in the end and dangles in the wind.
Always—I never knew it any other way—
The wind and the corn talk things over together.
And the rain and the corn and the sun and the corn
Talk things over together.

Over the road is the farmhouse.
The siding is white and a green blind is slung loose.
It will not be fixed till the corn is husked.
The farmer and his wife talk things over together.

Nebraska *Jon Swan*

There, there is no mountain within miles.
The land, slowly rising toward a distant glory,
Is devoid of ornaments or sudden splendor.
It is a land no tourist travels far to see.

Those who ride through it, hurrying to strong streams
Broken and shot across stones, or running to find
Gay palaces to possess the mind, hardly notice as they
    pass,
Or note with anger, the constant, level wind.

Yet this, the one companion of that land,
Might tell them, though they are always hurrying,
And though they hate that hot and wheat-high wind:
This was the bed of forgotten seas; this wheat is
    blossoming.

Grandpa's Trees

Barbara M. Hales

My grandpa built a farmhouse
Half a century ago.
On Arbor Day he planted trees
In one long tidy row.

He says they looked like beanpoles,
So leafless, frail, and small.
He tended them those early years
Though they gave no shade at all.

Today I counted forty trees
Tall-grown and sturdy-stout.
Their branches hug each other
As the wind blows them about.

They've sheltered Grandpa's farmhouse
In every sort of weather.
To me, they're friendly giants
Holding earth and sky together.

Sioux Lullaby   *Prince Redcloud*

Sleep, *mi su-la*,

little brother,

sleep,
sleep,
sleep,

Dream dreams, *mi su-la*,

little brother—

strong dreams,
brave dreams,
dreams so deep—

as you sleep, *mi su-la*,

little brother,

sleep,
sleep,
sleep.

Winter Dark   *Lilian Moore*

Winter dark comes early
mixing afternoon
and night.
Soon
there's a comma of a moon,

and each streetlight
along the
way
puts its period
to the end of day.

Now
a neon sign
punctuates the dark
with a bright
blinking
breathless
exclamation mark!

47

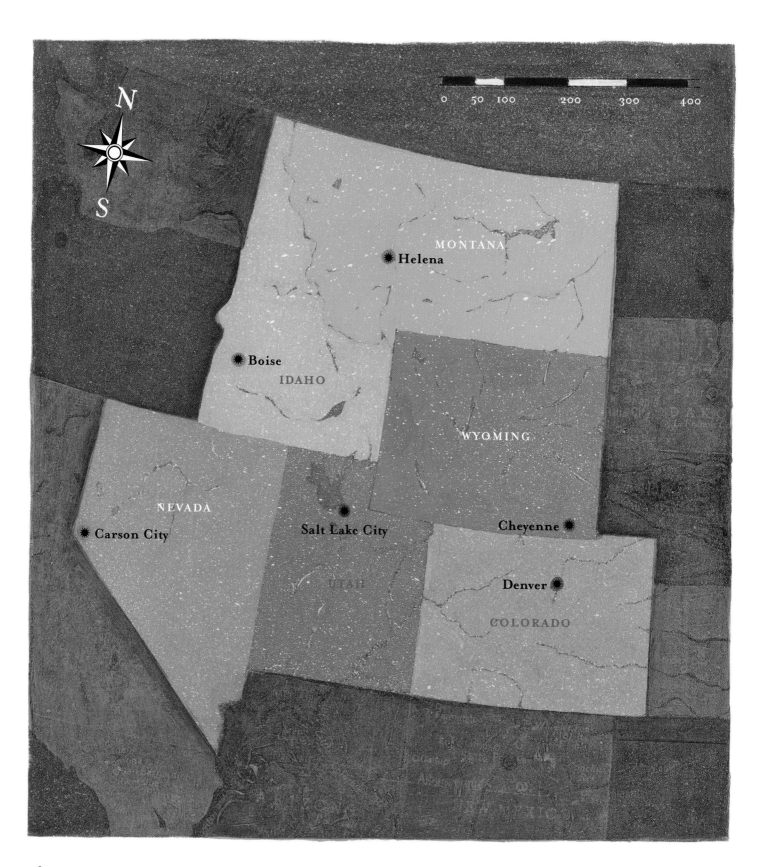

THE MOUNTAIN STATES

COLORADO

CO

On August 1, 1876, Colorado became the thirty-eighth state.

Capital: Denver
Nickname: Centennial State/Silver State
Motto: *Nil Sine Numine*
Nothing Without Providence
Bird: Lark Bunting
Flower: Rocky Mountain Columbine
Tree: Blue Spruce
Area: 104,100 square miles; rank 8

Great Fact:
The largest silver nugget ever found in North America was discovered in Aspen in 1894. It weighed 1,840 pounds and was 93 percent pure sterling silver.

IDAHO

ID

On July 3, 1890, Idaho became the forty-third state.

Capital: Boise
Nickname: Gem State/Potato State
Motto: *Esto Perpetua*
It Is Perpetual
Bird: Mountain Bluebird
Flower: Syringa
Tree: Western White Pine
Area: 83,574 square miles; rank 14

Great Fact:
Each year 27 billion potatoes are grown in Idaho—enough for every person in the United States to have about 100 potatoes per year.

MONTANA

MT

On November 8, 1889, Montana became the forty-first state.

Capital: Helena
Nickname: Treasure State
Motto: *Oro y Plata*
Gold and Silver
Bird: Western Meadowlark
Flower: Bitterroot
Tree: Ponderosa Pine
Area: 147,046 square miles; rank 4

Great Fact:
Each day about 390 million gallons of water gush out of the ground at Giant Springs in Great Falls. Aptly named, Giant Springs is among the largest freshwater springs in the world.

NEVADA

NV

On October 31, 1864, Nevada became the thirty-sixth state.

Capital: Carson City
Nickname: Sagebrush State/Battle Born State/Silver State
Motto: *All for Our Country*
Bird: Mountain Bluebird
Flower: Sagebrush
Tree: Single-Leaf Piñon/ Bristlecone Pine
Area: 110,567 square miles; rank 7

Great Fact:
Nevada's location in the Sierra Nevada rain shadow makes it the driest state in the country. Annual precipitation averages 9 inches, varying from 3 inches in the south to 29 inches in the Sierra Nevada. Most water is derived from mountain snow melt. Normal average precipitation: 7.5 inches.

UTAH

UT

On January 4, 1896, Utah became the forty-fifth state.

Capital: Salt Lake City
Nickname: Beehive State
Motto: *Industry*
Bird: Seagull
Flower: Sego Lily
Tree: Blue Spruce
Area: 84,904 square miles; rank 13

Great Fact:
In 1848, the seagull saved crops from an invasion of Mormon crickets. The Seagull Monument in Salt Lake City, unveiled in 1913, features sculptures of the state bird standing atop the monument.

WYOMING

WY

On July 10, 1890, Wyoming became the forty-fourth state.

Capital: Cheyenne
Nickname: Equality State
Motto: *Equal Rights*
Bird: Western Meadowlark
Flower: Indian Paintbrush
Tree: Cottonwood
Area: 97,819 square miles; rank 9

Great Fact:
Designated the country's first national monument in 1906, Devils Tower rises 1,280 feet from its base. Devils Tower was formed by an upsurge of molten lava millions of years ago in the Black Hills. In 1977, movie director Steven Spielberg used the setting for the spaceship landing in his classic science-fiction film *Close Encounters of the Third Kind*.

"For Purple Mountains' Majesty"   *Myra Cohn Livingston*

I saw them today.
I saw them.
So many years I have heard them in a song.
It's true. They're purple when you see them.
They rise like kings.
They are mountains.
Suddenly
I know.
I *really* know
What that song is all about.

50

Boulder, Colorado *X. J. Kennedy*

Skyscrapers made of earth—stones—trees
Take up as much sky as they please

And deck with white clouds, streams, wild flowers
Their top-floor observation towers.

Driving Montana   *Kris Aro McLeod*

Roll on highway, I'm goin' somewhere.
Window open, lettin' in bright air
of circling sky and mountains beyond,
the winding white lines lead me on.
Over bounding hills,
wheat whirls with joyful wind.
My shirt sleeves flap.
Freedom spins.

Idaho

Kaye Starbird

Farmers out in Idaho
Plant potatoes, row on row.
Then before the green vines show
Every farmer has to go
Daily hoe-ing with his hoe
Up and down the rows till—lo—
Finally potatoes grow.

This, potato farmers know:
What comes up must start below;
What you reap you have to sow;
What you grow you have to hoe.

If you don't like farming, though,
 And you've never *tried* a hoe
 Or you hate to guide a hoe
 Or you can't abide a hoe
 Stay away from Idaho.

Snow Country

Dave Etter

only
a little
yellow

school bus
creeping along
a thin

ribbon
of snow road
splashed color

on the white
winter canvas
that was

Wyoming
from the train
yesterday

Skier

Robert Francis

He swings down like the flourish of a pen
Signing a signature in white on white.

The silence of his skis reciprocates
The silence of the world around him.

Wind is his one competitor
In the cool winding and unwinding down.

On incandescent feet he falls
Unfalling, trailing white foam, white fire.

Zion National Park—Utah

Fran Haraway

Canyon walls remain unchanged by days,
Standing as they did when earth began.
Massive rock, passive to nature's ways
Unmoved by inquisitiveness of man.
Yet each evening brings a constant change.
Shadows quilt each hill and canyon wall.
Pastel patchworks gently rearrange
Antique patterns, then night covers all.

Until We Built a Cabin

Aileen Fisher

When we lived in a city
(three flights up and down)
I never dreamed how many stars
could show above a town.

When we moved to a village
where lighted streets were few,
I thought I could see ALL the stars,
but, oh, I never knew—

Until we built a cabin
where hills are high and far,
I never knew how many
            many
                stars there really are!

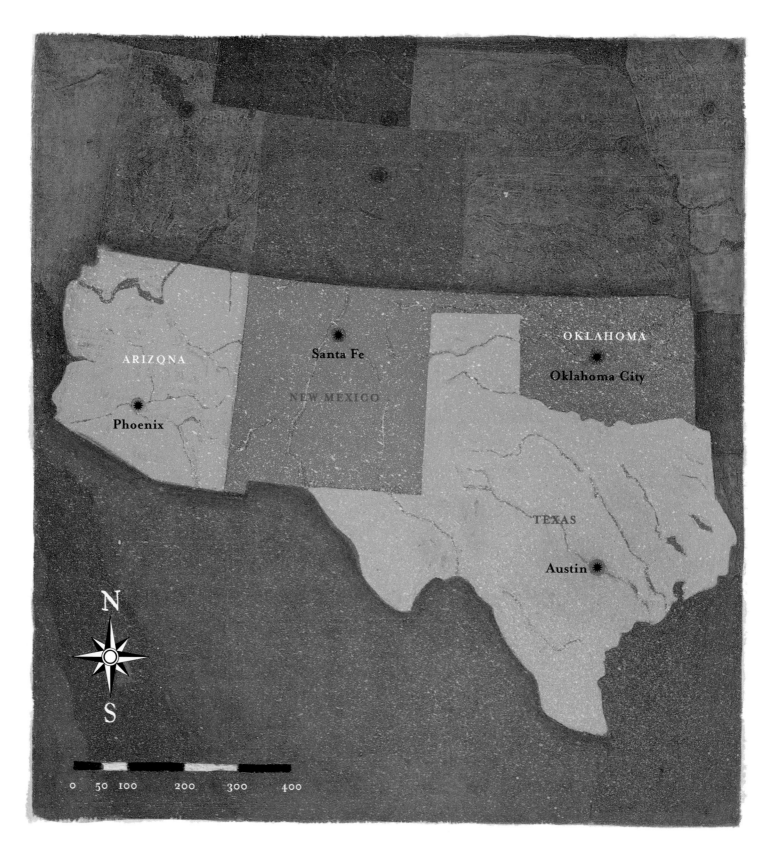

ARIZONA

On February 14, 1912, Arizona became the forty-eighth state.

Capital: Phoenix
Nickname: Grand Canyon State
Motto: *Ditat Deus*
God Enriches
Bird: Cactus Wren
Flower: Blossom of the Saguaro Cactus
Tree: Paloverde
Area: 114,006 square miles; rank 6

Great Fact:
The Grand Canyon on the Colorado River is the largest canyon in the world. It is nearly 1 mile deep, 4 to 18 miles wide, and about 277 miles long. One of the most popular tourist attractions in the United States, it is visited by nearly 4 million people annually.

NEW MEXICO

On January 6, 1912, New Mexico became the forty-seventh state.

Capital: Santa Fe
Nickname: Land of Enchantment
Motto: *Crescit Eundo*
It Grows as It Goes
Bird: Roadrunner
Flower: Yucca
Tree: Piñon Pine
Area: 121,598 square miles; rank 5

Great Fact:
Built as part of a fortress by the Spanish during the winters of 1609–1610, The Palace of the Governors, in Santa Fe, is the oldest government building in the United States. In 1909 it was converted to The Palace of the Governors History Museum, which now houses exhibits on Spanish, Mexican, and American colonization dating back to the late 1500s.

OKLAHOMA

On November 16, 1907, Oklahoma became the forty-sixth state.

Capital: Oklahoma City
Nickname: Sooner State
Motto: *Labor Omnia Vincit*
Labor Conquers All Things
Bird: Scissor-Tailed Flycatcher
Flower: Mistletoe
Tree: Redbud
Area: 69,903 square miles; rank 20

Great Fact:
Oklahoma is a major center of Native American culture. More than 60 different tribes live within the state, including the Arapaho, Cheyenne, Comanche, Osage, Pawnee, and Wichita. Oklahoma's name stems from two Choctaw Indian words—*okla*, meaning red, and *homma*, meaning people.

TEXAS

On December 29, 1845, Texas became the twenty-eighth state.

Capital: Austin
Nickname: Lone Star State
Motto: *Friendship*
Bird: Mockingbird
Flower: Bluebonnet
Tree: Pecan
Area: 267,277 square miles; rank 2

Great Fact:
The world's first coin-operated laundromat opened in Fort Worth on April 18, 1934, by J. F. Cantrell. It was called the Washateria.

Lifeline   *Shonto Begay*

Into the distance we ride
    Upon this road, gray and oily we ride
Toward the sacred mountain of the west
    Toward stories and songs of all-night ceremony
The roar of the wind in our ears
    The smell of fresh oil and sage clings to us.

We have seen ourselves on this road since childhood
    We have sat up front, we have sat in the back
We have felt the dry heat burning our lungs
    We have felt the chill of winter stinging our faces
We have laughed and we have cried upon this road
    We have left more than tire marks upon this road.

This is the lifeline of our land
This road which we travel day and night
This road that connects our communities,
Our families and our responsibilities.
Years from now—into the setting sun,
On this road we will still ride.

Cactus

April Halprin Wayland

"Don't dare come near,"
it says

with spike

with spear

with crossbow
poised to pierce . . .

beware!

Desert

Lillian M. Fisher

The desert is holding a giant breath
The air is dusty and dry
Red mesas shimmer in searing heat
Under a blanket of sky.

Coyote's asleep in slender shade
Dreaming of evening prey
For who would go out in a warm fur coat
To hunt on a summer day?
Lazy brown ants have made their retreat
To a colony under the hill
Tortoise and rabbit, even the birds
Are idle and peacefully still.

The desert is holding a giant breath
The air is dusty and dry
Red mesas shimmer in searing heat
Under a blanket of sky.

The Hawk

Douglas Florian

I stare
            I glare
I gaze
            I gawk
With keen
Mean eyes
I am the hawk.
All day I pray
For prey to view.
Be thankful if
I don't
see
YOU!

Santa Fe, New Mexico

April Halprin Wayland

up dusty red Canyon Road
in and out of art galleries
ducking out of the heat

into cool rooms filled with
pueblo paintings,
buffalo sculptures,
wrought iron Indians,

out again into the clear day
to see surprising piles of clouds,
melting, moving
mounds of white ice cream

look what I have found
out here
in *this* gallery.

March in New Mexico   *Elizabeth Coatsworth*

1

Coming home in the cold wind,
coming home through the sudden snow,
I thought, What if the fruit trees are not in blossom?
What if the birds have not yet come?
There is something inside me which is in blossom.
There is something inside me which lifts its head.

2

Walking with the Black Mesa beside me,
I said, I am glad that the mountains are hidden.
The clouds are low: we see only the hems of their
    garments,
patterned with snow. I am glad they are hidden.
Walking with the Black Mesa beside me
I said, It is better to feel the mountains very high,
very high and white behind the cloud banks.

3

The little horse is galloping. Quick, quick, he carries his
    rider.
They are going to the house of a girl,
the girl who lives by the river.
See how deep the hoofs cut into the sand!
See how close the hoof prints lie together!
The trail is a love poem, a little stanza which the desert
    wind will erase.

Grand Canyon Colors

Tom Robert Shields

Indian red.
Deep as orange earth.
Ever-changing sunlight
On rocks of blue hue.

Yellow layer after
Sun-splashed layer;
Burnt sienna burnt by the sun
For many, many turquoise years.

Violet-green swallows
Fly free
In solitude
Above
      and below
            a rainbow rim.

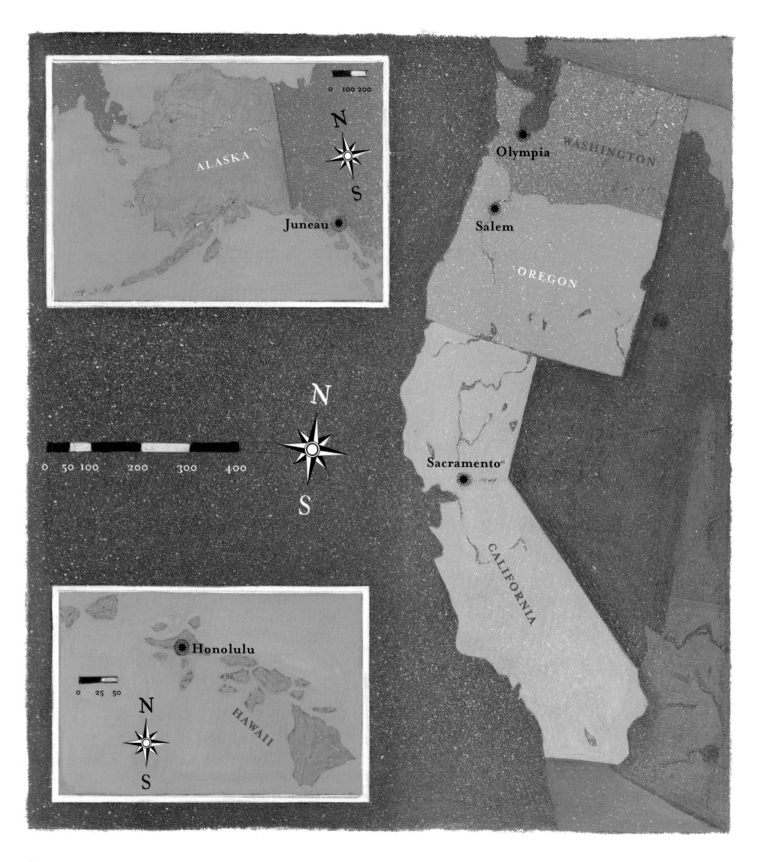

WASHINGTON

Olympia

Salem

OREGON

Sacramento

CALIFORNIA

ALASKA

Juneau

0 100 200

N
S

Honolulu

HAWAII

0   25 50

N
S

0 50 100   200   300   400

N
S

THE PACIFIC COAST STATES

ALASKA

On January 3, 1959, Alaska became the forty-ninth state.

Capital: Juneau
Nickname: The Last Frontier
Motto: *North to the Future*
Bird: Willow Ptarmigan
Flower: Forget-Me-Not
Tree: Sitka Spruce
Area: 615,230 square miles; rank 1

Great Fact:
Each winter more than 3,500 bald eagles gather along the Chilkat River just north of Haines, more than at any other place in the world. They come to this site to feed on late runs of salmon, which are accessible due to an unusual upwelling of warm water that keeps the river free of ice.

CALIFORNIA

On September 9, 1850, California became the thirty-first state.

Capital: Sacramento
Nickname: Golden State
Motto: *Eureka*
I Have Found It
Bird: California Quail
Flower: Golden Poppy
Tree: California Redwood
Area: 158,869 square miles; rank 3

Great Fact:
The General Sherman sequoia tree in Sequoia National Park is the largest single living thing on Earth. It weighs more than 6,167 tons—equal to 740 elephants or 41 blue whales. The oldest tree in the United States is a 4,700-year-old bristlecone pine in Inyo National Forest.

HAWAII

On August 21, 1959, Hawaii became the fiftieth state.

Capital: Honolulu
Nickname: Aloha State
Motto: *Ua Mau Ke Ea O Ka Aina I Ka Pono*
The Life of the Land Is Perpetuated in Righteousness
Bird: Nene (Hawaiian Goose)
Flower: Hibiscus
Tree: Kukui (Candlenut)
Area: 6,459 square miles; rank 47

Great Fact:
Mount Waialeale, on the island of Kauai, is one of the wettest places on Earth. The average yearly rainfall on the mountain is 460 inches.

OREGON

On February 14, 1859, Oregon became the thirty-third state.

Capital: Salem
Nickname: Beaver State/Sunset State
Motto: *Alis Volat Propriis*
She Flies with Her Own Wings
Bird: Western Meadowlark
Flower: Oregon Grape
Tree: Douglas Fir
Area: 97,093 square miles; rank 10

Great Fact:
Crater Lake is the deepest lake in the United States. It is 1,982 feet deep and is located at the top of a dead volcano.

WASHINGTON

On November 11, 1889, Washington became the forty-second state.

Capital: Olympia
Nickname: Evergreen State
Motto: *Alki*
By and By
Bird: Willow Goldfinch
Flower: Rhododendron
Tree: Western Hemlock
Area: 70,637 square miles; rank 19

Great Fact:
Father's Day, which was first celebrated on June 19, 1910, was originated by Sonora Louise Smart Dodd of Spokane.

California Missions

Ann Whitford Paul

They're tall and sturdy,
four feet thick,
built of stone
and mortar, brick.
Through quakes and plagues
each ancient wall
has stayed in place
and stood up tall.
No mouth to speak,
no ears to hear,
yet they hold tales
of ancient years.
I sit inside
and listen well
to every word
their silence tells.

California Ghost Town   *Fran Haraway*

Buildings blackened, boards warped, pushed askew
By winds and winter's harsh indifference. Through
Cracked, dust-patterned glass we see remains
Of safer, softer times before the stains
Decades create as they seek to reclaim
Their own, taking the heart, leaving the frame.
A spot forgotten as last autumn's news,
Yet, dusty streets show prints of tennis shoes!

Behind the Redwood Curtain

Natasha Wing

Redwood trees rise like skyscrapers
Fingering the clouds in search of moisture
Pulling down the fog and passing it
From limb to limb
Into the deep of the forest.
The fog blankets the forest
Blocking out light, movement, and sound
Like a curtain
Draped across a stage.
Yet behind the redwood curtain
Black bear walk and stalk their prey
Deer sleep and leap away
Slugs climb and slime on leaves
Birds sing and wing in the breeze.
The show must go on
As it has for thousands of years
Behind the redwood curtain.

Seattle Morning

Lee Bennett Hopkins

In the pouring
teeming rain

a deluge
pounding down
sounding
as if
it will
never
come to an
end again

a man
crouches
on the pavement
clutching a
bright yellow umbrella
in one hand
bending over
his

SEATTLE TIMES

intently
reading
today's
weather
report.

Alaska   *Joaquin Miller*

Ice built, ice bound, and ice bounded,
Such cold seas of silence! such room!
Such snow-light, such sea-light, confounded
With thunders that smite like a doom!
Such grandeur! such glory! such gloom!
Hear that boom! Hear that deep distant boom
Of an avalanche hurled
Down this unfinished world!

Ice seas! and ice summits! ice spaces
In splendor of white, as God's throne!
Ice worlds to the pole! and ice places
Untracked, and unnamed, and unknown!
Hear that boom! Hear the grinding, the groan
Of the ice-gods in pain! Hear the moan
Of yon ice mountain hurled
Down this unfinished world!

Mauna Loa

Tom Robert Shields

While Pacific Ocean's
White surf gleams
Rolling seas glide
Shifting dreams.

Sudden thunders—
A tumbled tune
Breaking lazy-beauty
Of a calm-quiet noon.

Birds of paradise scatter
As all birds do

Mauna Loa gulps—

Fire!

Long

over-

due.

ACKNOWLEDGMENTS

Every effort has been made to trace the ownership of all copyrighted material
and to secure necessary permissions to reprint these selections. In the event of any questions
arising as to the use of any material, the editor and the publisher, while expressing regret for
any inadvertent error, will be happy to make the necessary correction in future printings.
Thanks are due to the following for permission to reprint the selections below:

Curtis Brown, Ltd., for "New England Lighthouse," "This Is Indiana," "Washington, D.C." by Rebecca Kai Dotlich. Copyright © 2000 by Rebecca Kai Dotlich. "City Blockades" by Lee Bennett Hopkins. Copyright © 1972 by Lee Bennett Hopkins. "Kentucky," "Seattle Morning," "Wisconsin in Feb-b-rr-uary," by Lee Bennett Hopkins. Copyright © 2000 by Lee Bennett Hopkins. "Boulder, Colorado" from *The Forgetful Wishing Well* by X. J. Kennedy, published by Atheneum. Copyright © 1985 by X. J. Kennedy. All reprinted by permission of Curtis Brown, Ltd. ▌ Dave Etter for "Snow Country" from *Go Read the River* (University of Nebraska Press). Used by permission of the author, who controls all rights. ▌ Aileen Fisher for "Until We Built a Cabin" from *That's Why* (Thomas Nelson, Inc.). Copyright 1946 by Aileen Fisher. Used by permission of the author, who controls all rights. ▌ Lillian M. Fisher for "Desert." Used by permission of the author, who controls all rights. ▌ Barbara M. Hales for "Grandpa's Trees." Used by permission of the author, who controls all rights. ▌ Fran Haraway for "California Ghost Town," "Zion National Park—Utah." Used by permission of the author, who controls all rights. ▌ Harcourt Brace & Company for "Some Rivers" from *Sawgrass Poems: A View of the Everglades* by Frank Asch. Copyright © 1996 by Frank Asch. "The Hawk" from *On the Wing* by Douglas Florian. Copyright © 1996 by Douglas Florian. Excerpt from "Crossing Ohio When Poppies Bloom in Ashtabula" from *Good Morning, America* by Carl Sandburg. Copyright 1928 and renewed 1956 by Carl Sandburg. "Laughing Corn" from *Cornhuskers* by Carl Sandburg. Copyright 1918 by Holt, Rinehart and Winston and renewed 1946 by Carl Sandburg. All reprinted by permission of Harcourt Brace & Company. ▌ Lee Bennett Hopkins for "Farmer" and "Sioux Lullaby" by Prince Redcloud; "Grand Canyon Colors," "Mauna Loa," "The Mississippi" by Tom Robert Shields. Used by permission of Lee Bennett Hopkins for the authors, who control all rights. ▌ Kathryn Allen Ilitch for "Dear Cousin." Used by permission of the author, who controls all rights. ▌ Juliahouse Publishing Company for "Bourbon and Canal" from *Throw Me Somethin' Mistuh!* by Brod Bagert and Charles Smith. Copyright © 1995 by Brod Bagert and Charles Smith. Used by permission of Juliahouse Publishing Company. ▌ Alfred A Knopf, Inc., for "Alabama Earth (At Booker Washington's Grave)" from *Collected Poems* by Langston Hughes. Copyright © 1994 by the Estate of Langston Hughes. Reprinted by permission of Alfred A. Knopf, Inc. ▌ C. Drew Lamm for "Watercolor Maine." Used by permission of the author, who controls all rights. ▌ Anne LeMieux for "Gulls and Buoys." Used by permission of the author, who controls all rights. ▌ Little, Brown and Company for "Islands in Boston Harbor" from *One at a Time* by David McCord. Copyright © renewed 1980 by David McCord. By permission of Little, Brown, and Company. ▌ Kris Aro McLeod for "Driving Montana." Used by permission of the author, who controls all rights. ▌ William Morrow & Company, Inc., for "Knoxville, Tennessee" from *The Selected Poems of Nikki Giovanni*. Compilation copyright © 1996 by Nikki Giovanni. By permission of William Morrow & Company, Inc. ▌ New Directions Publishing Corporation for "Pine Tree Tops" from *Turtle Island* by Gary Snyder. Copyright © 1972, 1974 by Gary Snyder. Reprinted by permission of New Directions Publishing Corporation. ▌ The New England Press for "Frost's Farm Road" from *Uphill Home* by James Hayford. Copyright © 1992 by James Hayford. Reprinted by permission of The New England Press, Inc., Shelburne, Vermont. ▌ Ann Whitford Paul for "California Missions." Used by permission of the author, who controls all rights. ▌ Marian Reiner for "Vermont Conversation" from *The Apple Vendor's Fair* by Patricia Hubbell. Copyright © 1963 and renewed 1991 by Patricia Hubbell. "'For Purple Mountain's Majesty'" from *The Malibu and Other Poems* by Myra Cohn Livingston. Copyright © 1972 by Myra Cohn Livingston. "Winter Dark" from *I Thought I Heard the City* by Lilian Moore. Copyright © 1969 by Lilian Moore. Copyright © renewed 1997 by Lilian Moore Reavin. "Idaho" from *A Snail's a Failure Socially* by Kaye Starbird. Copyright © 1966 by Kaye Starbird. Copyright © renewed 1994 by Catherine D. Slawson. All reprinted by permission of Marian Reiner. ▌ The Saturday Evening Post Society for "Midwest Town" by Ruth De Long Peterson. Reprinted from *The Saturday Evening Post*. Copyright 1954. ▌ Scholastic, Inc., for "Lifeline" from *Navajo: Visions and Voices Across the Mesa* by Shonto Begay. Copyright © 1995 by Shonto Begay. Reprinted by permission of Scholastic, Inc. ▌ Simon & Schuster for "March in New Mexico" from *Down Half the World* by Elizabeth Coatsworth. Copyright 1949, 1968 by Elizabeth Coatsworth Beston. Copyright renewed 1976 by Elizabeth Coatsworth Beston. Reprinted with permission of Simon & Schuster Books for Young Readers, an imprint of Simon & Schuster Children's Publishing Division. "Nebraska" by Jon Swan from *Poets of Today, Vol. VII: Journeys and Returns: Poems*, edited by John Hall Wheelock. Copyright © 1960 by Jon Swan. Reprinted by permission of Scribner, a division of Simon & Schuster. ▌ The University of Massachusetts Press for "Skier" by Robert Francis from *Robert Francis: Collected Poems, 1936-1976*. (Amherst: The University of Massachusetts Press, 1976.) Copyright © 1965, 1976 by The University of Massachusetts Press. ▌ April Halprin Wayland for "Cactus," "Santa Fe, New Mexico." Used by permission of the author, who controls all rights. ▌ Natasha Wing for "Behind the Redwood Curtain." Used by permission of the author, who controls all rights.

INDEX OF AUTHORS

Anonymous   32

Asch, Frank   27

Bagert, Brod   24

Begay, Shonto   60

Coatsworth, Elizabeth   66

Dotlich, Rebecca Kai   8, 17, 31

Etter, Dave   54

Fisher, Aileen   57

Fisher, Lillian M.   63

Florian, Douglas   64

Francis, Robert   55

Giovanni, Nikki   23

Hales, Barbara M.   45

Haraway, Fran   56, 73

Hayford, James   11

Hopkins, Lee Bennett   10, 21, 34, 76

Hubbell, Patricia   12

Hughes, Langston   26

Ilitch, Kathryn Allen   33

Jennings, Leslie Nelson   35

Kennedy, X. J.   51

Lamm, C. Drew   5

Lechlitner, Ruth   41

LeMieux, Anne   9

Livingston, Myra Cohn   50

McCord, David   6

McLeod, Kris Aro   52

Miller, Joaquin   78

Moore, Lilian   47

Paul, Ann Whitford   72

Peterson, Ruth De Long   40

Redcloud, Prince   36, 46

Sandburg, Carl   30, 43

Shields, Tom Robert   25, 69, 79

Smith, Charles   24

Snyder, Gary   37

Starbird, Kaye   53

Swan, Jon   44

Wayland, April Halprin   61, 65

Wing, Natasha   74

INDEX OF TITLES

Alabama Earth   26
Alaska   78

Behind the Redwood Curtain   74
Boulder, Colorado   51
Bourbon and Canal   24

Cactus   61
California Ghost Town   73
California Missions   72
City Blockades   10
Crossing Ohio When Poppies Bloom
       in Ashtabula, *from*   30

Dear Cousin   33
Desert   63
Driving Montana   52

Farmer   36
"For Purple Mountains' Majesty"   50
Front Porch   35
Frost's Farm Road   11

Grand Canyon Colors   69
Grandpa's Trees   45
Gulls and Buoys   9

Hawk, The   64

Idaho   53
Islands in Boston Harbor   6

Kansas Boy   41
Kentucky   21
Knoxville, Tennessee   23

Laughing Corn   43
Lifeline   60

March in New Mexico   66
Mauna Loa   79
Midwest Town   40
Mississippi, The   25

Nebraska   44
New England Lighthouse   8

Pine Tree Tops   37

Santa Fe, New Mexico   65
Seattle Morning   76
Sioux Lullaby   46
Skier   55
Snow Country   54
Some Rivers   27

This Is Indiana   31
Tonight in Chicago   32

Until We Built a Cabin   57

Vermont Conversation   12

Washington, D.C.   17
Watercolor Maine   5
Winter Dark   47
Wisconsin in Feb-b-rr-uary   34

Zion National Park—Utah   56

INDEX OF FIRST LINES

B-rr, b-rr, b-rr, b-rr,   *34*

Buildings blackened, boards warped, pushed askew   *73*

Canyon walls remain unchanged by days,   *56*

Come on along—   *21*

Coming home in the cold wind,   *66*

Corner of Bourbon and Canal,   *24*

Dear Cousin: *33*

Deep in Alabama earth   *26*

"Don't dare come near,"   *61*

Farmers out in Idaho   *53*

Farther east it wouldn't be on the map—   *40*

"Good weather for hay."   *12*

Gulls swoop, gulls soar,   *9*

He swings down like the flourish of a pen   *55*

How many islands in the bay?   *6*

i always like summer   *23*

I feel so small   *10*

I pocketed a pebble   *11*

I saw them today.   *50*

I stare   *64*

Ice built, ice bound, and ice bounded,   *78*

in the blue night   *37*

In the pouring   *76*

Indian red.   *69*

Into the distance we ride   *60*

It's a sitting-pretty, windy-city kind of a place.   *32*

It's a tower   *8*

My grandpa built a farmhouse   *45*

On the east bank of the Potomac,   *17*

only   *54*

People who live in cities never know   *35*

Pick me poppies in Ohio,   *30*

Redwood trees rise like skyscrapers   *74*

Roll on highway, I'm goin' somewhere.   *52*

Skyscrapers made of earth—stones—trees   *51*

Sleep, *mi su-la*,   *46*

Some rivers rush to the sea.   *27*

The buoy bell sings Bar Harbor   *5*

The desert is holding a giant breath   *63*

The farmer, worn from   *36*

There, there is no mountain within miles.   *44*

There was a high majestic fooling   *43*

They're tall and sturdy,   *72*

This is Indiana,   *31*

This Kansas boy who never saw the sea   *41*

Two thousand   *25*

up dusty red Canyon Road   *65*

When we lived in a city   *57*

While Pacific Ocean's   *79*

Winter dark comes early   *47*